Dr. Gwen's
A to Z Self-Care Guide
for TEENS

SMILE, SHINE, SHARE

Gwendolyn A. Martin, Ed.D., LPC

Also by Dr. Gwen

LIVE YOUR BEST LIFE

(Journal)

Copyright © 2021 by Gwendolyn A. Martin

Library of Congress Control Number: 2021912761

ISBN-13: 978-1-7364413-3-6

Dedication

This book is dedicated to every TEEN who aspires to SMILE, SHINE, and SHARE their awesomeness.

My Message

Let me start by being honest. Being a teenager is tough. There will be times when nothing will go your way, and it seems like there's a dark cloud hanging over your head. You will feel alone, friends will desert and disappoint you, parents won't understand you, your schedule at school will suck and you won't make the team.

Trust me, I've been there. It's easy to feel defeated and get sucked into a place of uncertainty, fear, self-pity, and doubt. I'm here to tell you don't do it. Love yourself and smile right through it. I know you have heard the saying "fake it until you make it". This too, shall pass.

The sun WILL shine again. You will realize you are not alone. You will discover who your REAL friends are or make new ones. Your parents will finally give you the independence and freedom you've been fighting to obtain. You will pass algebra despite almost losing your freaking mind. Not only will you make the team, but you will be the captain and score the winning shot right at the buzzer. Ok, maybe I got a little carried away, but heck anything is possible.

Practicing **SELF-CARE** routinely is how you will persevere through the tough teenage years and not let ANYTHING block your shine. Let's go!

Introduction

I am super-duper excited to share Dr. Gwen's A to Z Self-Care Guide for Teens. Teenagers face a tremendous amount of pressure from parents, peers, and society. Academics, extracurricular activities, and family dynamics are just a few pressures you must navigate. Let's not forget you are trying to figure out who you are, who your REAL friends are, where you fall on the social continuum and all the ups and downs that come with growth and development. This includes hormonal changes (pimples, growth spurts [weight and height]), mood swings along with self-image and self-esteem struggles exacerbated by social media. If that isn't enough, you are trying to gain more independence and discover ways to express your true authentic self. Needless to say, the teenage years can be a very confusing, stressful, overwhelming time in your life.

This book contains some powerful, effective, practical self-care tips and solutions that can easily be incorporated into your existing daily routine. Self-care is all about engaging in deliberate activities and practices on a regular basis to reduce stress and respond better to difficult situations. Self-care will help you engage in more activities that make you feel happy, connected, and supported. As a result, you will give your physical, mental, and emotional health a boost.

Focus on making small improvements. Each change you make moves you closer to living your best life. Dr. Gwen's Self-Care Tips included throughout the book will help. Practice these tips and share them with your family and friends.

I'm here to support you on this self-care journey. Let's make a commitment to start living your best life TODAY! I'll be cheering you onevery step of the way. YOU GOT THIS!

Smile-Shine-Share, Dr. Gwen

Contents

SELF

Change your mindset and attitude.

Ask for help when needed.

Rest, release, recharge, and renew.

Eat healthy and exercise regularly.

IT'S A BRAND NEW DAY!

Today is a new beginning. Together we are going to make sure that you SMILE, SHINE, and SHARE all your awesomeness during these crazy tumultuous teenage years. As you embark on this SELF-CARE journey, the first thing we are going to do is highlight some of your positive character traits and qualities. That's right, toot your own horn, throw some confetti, and shine a light on YOU! Why you ask? Because **YOU ARE AWESOME!** I want to make sure you know it. For some of you it might take a little, (well a lot of convincing) but I'm up for the challenge.

Next, we will write an **affirmation** statement. Affirmations are positive statements that can help you to overcome self-sabotaging, negative thoughts. You SHOULD recite your affirmation daily to help reprogram your subconscious mind. You **ARE** smart enough, pretty/handsome enough, and deserve to be healthy and happy. Let me say it again, **YOU ARE AWESOME!**

Place a picture of yourself that you love in the frame and surround it with words that highlight your character, interest, strengths, and that make you different and unique...authentically YOU!

DON'T BLOCK MY SHINE!

My Positive Affirmation Statement

Fill in the blanks with positive traits and strengths.

Look out and stand back. Here comes_____.

Your Name

Dang, she/he is so_____. Did you know

Positive Trait

_____is_____,

Your Name	Positive Trait

and_____. She/he is also an extremely

Positive Trait

talented_____. For example,

One of Your Best Traits

_____

Example of the Positive Trait in action

_____

_____

I am so freaking AWESOME!

READ THIS ALOUD DAILY!

Embrace your

DNA

Heritage

Name

Religion

Style

UNIQUENESS.

A

Be STRONG enough

to stand alone,

SMART enough

to know when you need help

and

BRAVE enough to ASK for it.

A – Ask For Help

Asking for help is a hard thing for many of us to do. However, asking for help is a healthy natural response to challenging situations. It's important for you to realize that you are human, will make mistakes, and that you can't do everything alone. Cut yourself some slack. Try to keep things in perspective. Don't put too much pressure on yourself. There are people who want to help you, who will help you, all you got to do is ask. You do not have to struggle with difficult situations on your own. Seek help, guidance, support, and ideas from parents, mentors, teachers, counselors, coaches, and others in your community. Give your family and friends a chance to help.

Psst! Want to know a secret?

Parents love when you make them feel needed by asking for their help or opinion. You know they think they know it all. Well in some cases they do but we won't tell them.

Dr. Gwen's Self-Care Tip:

Make a list of people you can ask for help and call on for support. Asking for help is one of the bravest moves you can make. It means you won't have to face the problem alone no matter how big or small it may seem.

Family:

Friends:

Spiritual Leaders:

Mentors:

Coaches:

Community Leaders:

Counselors:

When asking for help, be direct and specific about what you need. Communicate what you have done to try to solve the problem yourself first. People are more apt to help you if they know that you are trying to help yourself.

Examples:

I have a research paper due on_____and I am having trouble narrowing down a topic. Will you help me?

I hate Math. There are some concepts that I just don't get. Last year I barely passed despite spending hours on homework and studying for tests. Do you know any tutoring programs? I can't spend another year like last year.

I haven't been getting much sleep lately. I go to bed at a decent time, I'm not on the phone or up watching TV but hours later I'm still wide awake. Have you ever had problems falling and staying asleep?

My friend_____and I had a fight. Lately we haven't been getting along. It's stressing me out. I'm not sure what the problem is. Can you tell me what you think?

Lately I seem tired all the time. I feel like I get enough sleep but when I wake up, I still feel exhausted. I can barely stay awake in class. My teachers probably think I'm lazy, don't care or stay up all night but that is not the case. Do you know why I'm feeling so tired all the time?

It is important to find someone to talk to about your feelings. Talking about your feelings is a healthy self-care strategy. Let others help you get unstuck, find solutions to your problems, and start feeling happier again.

Don't ever think you are asking for too much. If you don't get the desired results the first, second, or third time you ask someone, keep asking until you get the desired results. You may have just asked the wrong people.

If you or someone you love is struggling,

PLEASE

reach out and ask someone for help.

We are here for you.

You are not alone!

B

If you get tired,

learn to take

BRAIN BREAKS,

<u>don't</u> quit.

B – Brain Breaks

First, what is a brain break? Simply stated, a brain break is a mental or physical activity that helps re-energize and re-engage the brain. Brain breaks help to soothe the mind, settle fidgeting, minimize disruptive behavior, improve concentration, and reduce stress and anxiety. We could all benefit from taking brain breaks routinely or when the need arises to destress and manage our emotions. Check out *Dr. Gwen's Brain Break Kit* for kids at drgwenscounselorcafe.com/shop.

Follow these two steps to give brain breaks a try while doing homework or dreaded tasks.

1. Use a Timer

Setting a timer is a great way to remind yourself to take a mental break. Timers will also help keep you on track. Try scheduling a three to five minute brain break every 20 to 30 minutes and adjust the time as needed. Set the timer at the start of your task for 20 to 30 minutes. When the timer goes off, stop, and take a brain break.

At the start of your break set the timer for three to five minutes to remind you to get back to work.

Now go ahead and knock the rest of your assignment out. Each task or assignment you complete will help you feel a sense of accomplishment (especially for those hard to do task) and is helping to build your self- confidence, self-esteem, and resilience.

2. Break Assignments into Manageable Parts

You can also plan breaks around tasks instead of using a timer. Start by breaking your tasks into shorter manageable parts. For Example, if you have 20 math problems for homework, you might decide to take a break after completing the first five or ten.

If you get stuck, frustrated or your attention starts to fade before getting to the desired number, go ahead, and take a break.

However, if you are on a roll, you may want to just keep going and get it done. You be the judge.

Here is a list of short three to five minute brain break ideas. Consider your personality as you pick from the list. Are you someone who enjoys quiet time, or are you someone who would rather get up and move?

- Rubik's cube
- Spinners
- Yoga poses
- Doddle/Sketch pad
- Play with your pet
- Eat a healthy snack
- Get up and stretch
- Relax – Close your eyes and take deep breaths

I know you have a lot of stressors in your life like school, sports, clubs, recitals and maybe even a job. Even things you enjoy can be stressful when your plate is full. Sometimes we get so busy doing things that we **MUST** do that we stop doing things we **WANT** to do that make us happy.

Dr. Gwen's Self-Care Tip:

Make a list of five hobbies and activities you enjoy or would like to try the next time you take a break. Remember, these brain break activities will help minimize stress.

1.

2.

3.

4.

5.

BRAIN BREAKS

Read a book
Go for a walk
Journal
Cook/Bake
Draw or color
Blow bubbles
Garden
Write a letter
Listen to music
Take a nap
Play with a pet
Go fishing
Play a game
Play an instrument
Scrapbook
Complete a puzzle
Visit a museum.
Volunteer
Paint your nails.
Write poetry
Visit a friend
Make origami

Sometimes you need to

TAKE A BREAK

from the noise

to remind yourself

who you are

and who you want to BECOME.

YOU ARE AWESOME!

C

Communication must be **HOT!**

Honest

Open

and **T**wo-Way.

— *Dan Oswald*

C – Communication Is Key

Communicate your wants and needs, then ask yourself if what you are doing is helping to bring you closer to fulfilling that need or moving you further away. Communicate your thoughts and feelings to help others understand how you perceive the world so that they can better understand you and know how to help you. Communication is the key to success and getting what you want out of life. Learn to do it effectively. It is one of the best ways to build and maintain strong, healthy relationships.

As you grow up, having good communication skills will help you gain the independence you so desperately seek. The way you communicate with your parents and other adults will need to reflect the shift in new boundaries such as appearances, personal space, curfews, friends, and freedoms. Although parents often say they know what you are thinking they really can't read your mind. It is your responsibility to communicate what you need.

Effective communication will help you obtain your wants and needs, feel happier, and stay connected to the people that mean the most to you. **Good communication skills will also help you feel more confident and prepared when it is time to have those difficult, uncomfortable, complicated, conversations with real consequences, like school, friends, driving and let's not forget**

about substance use and sex. There will be times when you won't see eye-to-eye with others, and you will need to resolve conflicts with your parents and even your friends. Effective communication will help you make more informed decisions and avoid engaging in risky behavior.

Dr. Gwen's Self-Care Tip:

Here are some tips that can help you have positive and constructive interactions with others, especially your parents who just don't understand (pun intended)! ☺

Practicing these effective communication strategies are sure to help you avoid roadblocks and gain access to your wants and needs.

1. Find an optimal time

One of the biggest mistakes kids make when communicating their desires is doing it at the wrong time. Finding time to talk can be difficult when everyone's schedule is super busy. However, don't wait until the last minute to ask permission to do something that you already know your parents will more than likely not have time to really consider. If they feel ambushed the answer is generally going to be NO.

Car rides can be an excellent way to strike up a conversation and express your wants and needs. One of the good things about riding in a car is that you don't have to make eye contact. Car rides may give you the extra kick in the butt and opportunity to comfortably bring up uncomfortable subjects or put in those requests.

It is better to ask permission in advance. By doing so, your parents will have time to consider your request without immediately having to say no because you didn't give them time to consider all the factors that come along with your request. For example, if you want to attend an event with a friend don't spring this information on your parents at the last minute while they are rushing out the door, especially if it is a friend that your parents have never met.

Let me warn you. Your parents will probably interrogate the hell out of you by rapidly firing off questions. **Don't worry, YOU GOT THIS!** Go ahead and provide as much information as you can up front. For Goodness Sakes, do your homework before you approach them. Otherwise, your NO will come sooner than later.

Here are some potential questions and things to consider:

How do you know this friend?

How long have you been friends?

Why haven't your parents met this friend?

Where does your friend live?

Who are your friend's parents and what do they do?

Where is the event?

How will you and your friend get to and from the event?

What time will the event end?

Who will attend the event?

Will there be chaperones?

Please understand that there will probably be additional questions your parents will ask depending on the subject matter or request. Don't get frustrated by your parents need to know and understand every aspect of a situation. **Their primary job is to keep you safe.**

This is an optimal time to show how mature and responsible you are by staying calm and effectively communicating your request by answering all their questions. Even if the outcome is a **BIG FAT NO**, take a deep breath, count to 10, control your emotions and rejoice in the fact that you have earned some major points with your parents by being proactive, not waiting until the last minute and remained calm despite being disappointed. You will also have gained some valuable insight in to how your parents think and the reasons they said no. You can then go to your room and cry or better yet journal about the experience and your disappointment. There is always next time and next time you will be better prepared.

2. Give the speaker your undivided attention.

Choose a quiet space free of distractions when you need to have important conversations. In other words, put the phone or game controller down. Better yet, turn them off. While you're at it, turn the TV off too so you can give your undivided attention and you will have theirs also. Interruptions and distractions make it harder to keep your train of thought and get your point across.

3. Listen

Take time to listen to your parents without jumping in or being argumentative. It's hard. Trust me, I know but you can do hard things. Listen to understand their feelings and concerns.

Your parents have been where you are and MOST of their concerns are valid. **A parent's worst nightmare is losing YOU.** They really don't want to make your life miserable but if it means protecting you from potential hurt, harm, or danger, they will choose miserable YOU every time. It's an easy choice for them to make.

By taking time to listen to your parents' concerns and effectively communicating your wants, hopefully you will be able to come to a mutual compromise that everybody can live with by better understanding each other's point of view.

Additional Tips:

Please pay close attention to your **nonverbal "body language"** during communication. In some instances, what comes out of your mouth and what you communicate nonverbally may convey two totally different things. If you say one thing, but your body language says something totally different, you may appear dishonest or unsure. For example, saying "yes" while shaking your head no. Another example would be saying you agree and understand but rolling your eyes. Those eyes can get you in **BIG trouble**. When you give off mixed signals, your nonverbal message is believed instead of what you say because you are providing a visual display of your true feeling and intentions.

I've listed a few nonverbals for you to consider below.

1. Facial Expressions

The way your eyes, nose and mouth convey what you are thinking or feeling.

Yeah, that smirk probably isn't going to work in your favor.

2. Posture

The way you stand or sit, also the position of your shoulders and chin.

Sit up straight and tall and do not slouch. If you want to be treated like an adult, act like one.

3. Gestures

How you use your arms, legs, and head to say things.

Uncross those arms and you better not point that finger.

Your body communicates

as well as your mouth.

Don't contradict yourself.

— Allen Ruddock

D

Think Big

DREAM BIG

Believe Big

and the Results

Will Be Big

D – Dream BIG.

Michael Phelps the most successful and most decorated Olympian of all time said "You dream. You plan. You reach. There will be obstacles. There will be doubters. There will be mistakes. But with hard work, with belief, with confidence and trust in yourself and those around you, there are no limits."

Your teenage years will be a great time to get serious about your goals and start thinking about your future career if you haven't already. Finding your purpose and engaging in meaningful activities comes easily for some teenagers and not so easily for others.

Complete the activity sheet on the next page to start exploring a future career. Visit moneyprodigy.com a free career exploration site for kids for additional information and interactive activities.

Dr. Gwen's Self-Care Tip:

Find a Mentor.

Find a successful family member or community leader who has the kind of job you are interested in. Ask this person if they are willing to share their work experience, skills, training, career path, opinions, and suggestions about the job with you. Most adults will be more than willing to lend a helping hand to an AWESOME, aspiring, motivated teen like YOU. Having a mentor can significantly broaden your career opportunities.

DREAM BIG

Future Career:

What got you interested in this career and why do you think you would be good at it?

Education needed:

Skills needed:

List 3 things you could do to prepare for this career.

1.

2.

3.

What questions do you have about this career?

E

Express yourself through your art – whether it's your drawings in a sketchpad, tattoos on your skin, the shade of your lipstick, or the clothes that you wear.

— Kat Von D

E — Express Yourself

Creative expression provides an opportunity to release complicated emotions through music, journaling, visual arts, poetry, dance, or hobbies. Extracurricular activities that evoke a sense of peace and calm can be extremely effective for reducing stress during the teen years.

You might feel pressured to fit in with peers and feel uncomfortable expressing your talents, uniqueness, and individual preferences. That's why creative expression and authenticity is so powerful and important. Expressing your emotions through an art form can be fun and helps to minimize adverse thought and feelings.

Dr. Gwen's Self-Care Tip:

Here are two ways to express yourself. I left some room for you to share how you express yourself currently and something new you would like to try. There are unlimited possibilities.

The Arts

The creative arts are an easy way to express and communicate your feelings in a variety of ways. Studies have shown that Art therapy can improve your physical, mental, and emotional well-being. The arts can include writing, painting, poetry, music, dancing, and performing. Be open to trying different art forms and exploring various forms of artistic expression. You might just be the next big phenomenon.

Be a Trend Setter

Fashion designer Marc Jacobs once said, "To me, clothing is a form of self-expression — there are hints about who you are in what you wear." Your personal style choices are a way to display self-expression without having to say one mumbling word.

What you wear may say a lot about your personality, attractiveness, femininity/masculinity, values, or culture. Be confident and unique in your style choices. Wear whatever makes you feel good. Ralph Lauren summed it up best when he said "Fashion is not necessarily about labels. It's not about brands. It's about something else that comes from within you."

Something I Do Currently To Express Myself

Something New I Would Like To Try

F

Failure

is a part of

success.

Fail

until you

succeed.

F – Failure Is an Opportunity for Improvement.

Is the fear of failure keeping you from taking risks and stepping outside your comfort zone? Fear of failure can be debilitating. We need to stop viewing failure as a measure of our worth, a sign of weakness, or an indication that we are not competent. Get back up, dust yourself off, and try again. Let's start viewing failure as a chance to start over and do things better. Successful people view failure as learning and growth opportunities. They are transparent and open to sharing that they got it wrong many times before finally getting it right. They share how they capitalized on their failures and did not give up when they encountered roadblocks and setbacks. Don't let failure stop you from accomplishing your dreams.

Dr. Gwen's Self-Care Tip:

Michael Jordan is undoubtedly one of the greatest basketball players of all time. Did you know that he started as a kid who couldn't make the junior varsity team? He started out as a kid that wasn't that good. However, when he set expectations for himself, he became arguably the greatest player in history.

Questions to consider after a failure:

1. Are my expectations/goals realistic?

I know you have heard the saying you must crawl before you walk. You can't start out running. In other words, sometimes we set our initial goals too high and don't give ourselves the time or grace we need to succeed. Cut yourself some slack. Break your goals down into smaller more achievable pieces.

2. What can I do differently?

Take time to reflect on what went well and what was an epic failure. This is just a minor setback. Think about what you can do differently the next time around. Knowledge is power. Small tweaks and changes can make a world of difference.

3. Do I have a growth mindset?

Are your vibes positive or is negative self-talk keeping you grounded in fear and doubt? Monitor your thought life. For example, don't say things like I can't do this... I'm not good enough or smart enough...I suck! Instead, tell yourself that you are getting a little better each day. Remember failure is an opportunity for improvement.

4. Who can help?

Have you asked for help or better yet, have you asked for help from the right person? Find someone who has done what you are trying to do and ask them for suggestions and support. They should be able to help you create a plan specific to your needs and goals.

G

Cultivate an

attitude

of

GRATITUDE.

G – Gratitude

What is gratitude? Simply stated, gratitude is one of many positive emotions. It's about focusing on what's good in our lives and being thankful for the things we have, rather than what we don't have. Expressing gratitude instantly shifts your mindset from being negative and self-defeating to positive and appreciative.

Gratitude means taking time to acknowledge the things that we often take for granted, like a roof over our heads, food to eat, family and friends who love and care about us and yes, even computer and phone access. It's taking a moment to pause and reflect on how blessed, thankful, lucky, fortunate, or humbled we are for things big and small.

Dr. Gwen's Self-Care Tip:

Studies show that making gratitude part of your daily life boosts psychological health, enhances empathy, reduces stress, lowers depression, and improves self-esteem. A study led by Martin Seligman, known as the father of positive psychology, found that a one-time act of thoughtful gratitude produced an immediate 10% increase in happiness and 35% reduction in depressive symptoms. That's the power of gratitude.

How to Practice Gratitude

Here are three ways to strengthen and flex your gratitude muscle daily and cultivate an attitude of gratitude.

1. Begin and end the day with gratitude.

When you get out of bed every morning, say three things you are grateful for and looking forward to during the day.

Before going to bed at night, write in a gratitude journal. As expressing gratitude states becomes a habit, you will find yourself acknowledging and expressing gratitude throughout the day.

2. Write positive reviews for influencers you follow.

Use your favorite social media platforms to review or highlight people who inspire you! Tell them how and why you follow and appreciate their work. Share their work with others so they can be inspired too.

3. Show Your Appreciation

Show your appreciation to someone who did something nice by writing a letter or giving them a thank you card. Here are some ways you can start. Say: "I can't thank you enough for...," "It really helped me out when you...," "Thank you for being there when....".

Think about the people, places, things, and events you are grateful for and place them inside your "Gratitude Jar". When you are feeling down, look in your jar and reflect on all the things that make you feel happy, loved, and appreciated.

H

Hug Someone!

One hug from

the right person

can take all your

stress away.

H – Hug Someone

Hugging is good for your mind, body, and soul. There is something about the physical contact hugs provide that is soothing, reassuring, comforting, calming, uplifting, and stress-reducing. When you give or get a hug, there is a transfer of positive energy that provides an immediate emotional "pick-me-up".

Scientists say that hugging is a great way to communicate what you can't always express in words. For example, a hug may say I'm sorry, I love you, forgive me, I'm here for you etc.

I know some of you won't readily admit that you enjoy hugs as much as the rest of us, but hugging is important at any age and the teenage years are no exception. Everyone needs a hug every now and then. Many studies have been conducted about a hug's remarkable healing power. Huggers tend to be healthier and happier people.

How many hugs do we need and how long should they last?

Researchers say:

- We need **four** hugs a day for survival.

- We need **eight** hugs a day for maintenance.

- We need **twelve** hugs a day for growth.

- Hugs should last at least **six** seconds.

- **Twenty** second hugs have medical healing properties.

So, the next time you feel sad, lonely, or depressed asking for a hug is a good place to start feeling better. A little squeeze may be just what is needed to reduce your stress, improve communication, and be happier. Start by asking for hugs from friends and family members closest to you. Wouldn't it be great if we could just hug out all our problems?

Dr. Gwen's Self-Care Tip:

Sometimes you just
need a
HUG...
no words,
no advice,
just a hug
to make you
feel
you matter.

I

Sometimes

the greatest gift

you can give someone

is to simply

invite and include them.

I – Invite and Include Others

Find ways to invite and include others to increase your learning opportunities so that you continue to grow and expand your knowledge and understanding of other cultures. This diverse world in which we live is a beautiful thing. Make a lifelong commitment to invest in YOU by dedicating time and energy to your personal development by embracing differences.

Inviting and including others is a great way to make and strengthen friendships. Clubs, youth groups, sports or community events are great ways to ask others to join in.

Inviting friends over for parties, backyard barbeques, to play games or watch movies, if your home situation allows, is another way to strengthen relationships.

Physical activities like bike riding, hiking, tossing around the football, kicking the soccer ball, or shooting a round of hoops may be your preferred method of socializing.

Dr. Gwen's Self-Care Tip:

Write down three to five ways you will start inviting and including others. This simple gesture and act of kindness can make a huge difference in someone's day. Author, Dana Arcuri reminds us that our job on earth isn't to criticize, reject, or judge. Our purpose is to offer a helping hand, compassion, and mercy.

1.

2.

3.

4.

5.

When everyone is included, everyone wins. ~ *Jessie Jackson*

J

I can shake off
everything as I write,
my sorrows disappear,
my courage is reborn.

— Anne Frank

J – Journal (Gratitude, Reflection, Mood, Drawing).

Journaling is a great way to get your feeling and emotions out. It is recommended for anyone, from children to adults, who want to relax, become more grateful, get to know themselves better, train their thoughts, prioritize problems, fears, concerns, and set goals in a judgment-free zone.

If you are a teenager who is experiencing complicated emotions, stress, loneliness, or depression writing in a journal is a great way to release and purge those self-defeating and sabotaging thoughts and feelings. There are many types of journals to choose from: gratitude, reflection, mood, drawing, affirmations, poetry, and the list goes on and on. Some people prefer to keep multiple journals, while others prefer keeping all their thoughts in one place. Do what works best for you. The journal you're most likely to use regularly is what I recommend.

One of the ways I practice self-care and invest in myself daily is by journaling before I go to bed. I started journaling during my teenage years and it has become a treasured practice. I find that I am more focused on my goals when I get my thoughts and feelings out of my head and on paper. Journaling brings clarity to my thoughts, feelings, and aspirations. It makes me feel more in control.

Journaling also helps me stop, self-reflect, and it provides an emotional space to express love, gratitude, and compassion. It is rewarding when I look back and see how much I have changed for the better and how many goals I've accomplished.

Dr. Gwen's Self-Care Tip:

Here are a few prompts to get your journal writing started. I also recommend picking up *Dr. Gwen's Live Your Best Life Journal.* It is a combination of many of the journals I reference above and may help you determine which kind works best for you.

What is the most inspiring thing you've ever heard?

_____

_____

_____

_____

_____

What freedom/privilege are you looking forward to as an adult?

_____

_____

_____

_____

_____

What is the hardest thing you've ever had to do?

_____

_____

_____

_____

_____

How do you feel at this very moment?

_____

_____

_____

_____

_____

What is your proudest accomplishment?

_____

_____

_____

_____

_____

K

Being KIND

costs nothing,

but means

EVERYTHING!

K – Kindness Matters

Kindness is caring for others, even when they may not care for you. It's about treating others with respect and compassion.

Research shows that kindness is linked to increased peer acceptance, improved academic performance, and positive mental health. It pays to be kind. Don't let the social pressures of being a teenager turn you in to a mean girl, bully or someone who excludes others. Be reminded of what you just read about inviting and including others under letter- I.

I challenge and encourage you to do random acts of kindness for others. It can be something as simple as smiling at another person as they pass by, taking time to play a game or read to your bratty younger sibling, or standing up for someone if they are being bullied. Don't be a bystander. No one deserves to be bullied. If you see something, say something, even if it's anonymous.

Random acts of kindness may seem small in the grand scheme of things, but they can instantly brighten a person's day. It will brighten yours too. I love to cook and occasionally take food to work to share with colleagues. I also drop food off to elderly family members or invite friends over for dinner. I love seeing the smiles of appreciation and anticipation on their faces. It makes me feel good to make someone else's day, especially if I had a lousy one. The good feelings that come from helping others are linked to emotional well-being. Studies have found that many people experience a rush of endorphins, often called a "helper's high," when they are kind to others.

Dr. Gwen's Self-Care Tip:

Think of ways you can show kindness at school, at home, to yourself, to friends and in your community.

Here are a few ideas to get you started.

1. Give someone a high-five, fist pump, or pat on the back.

2. Ask someone about their day.

3. Give compliments.

4. Complete someone's chore.

5. Show empathy.

6. Learn about other cultures.

7. Use positive self-talk.

8. Walk a neighbor's dog.

9. Let someone else pick what to watch on TV.

10. Donate your allowance to a charity.

L

The capacity to learn is a **gift**;

the ability to learn is a **skill**;

the willingness to learn is a

choice.

— Brian Herbert

L – Learn a New Skill or Hobby.

When was the last time you did something for the first time? Be the person who is full of energy and enthusiasm to learn a new skill or hobby. Find something significant that brings love and light into your life. You should have at least one skill or hobby that you are passionate about and look forward to doing regularly.

Here are some things to consider. Answer the questions below to get your creative juices flowing and spark new interest. Do not let fear of the unknown or a lack of knowledge or skills hold you back. You can do anything you set your mind to if you are willing to put in some work. The important thing is to have fun, challenge your brain, open your mind to new ideas and be willing to take risks.

In the summer of 2020 during the height of the pandemic, I was asked to participate in an anthology. Mind you, I've read hundreds of books but never considered being a writer. However, I decided that I would be willing to try because it was a book about women empowerment and a great opportunity. Fast forward to one year later. To date, I've written chapters for two anthologies and a textbook, and self-published my first book, **_Dr. Gwen's A to Z Self-Care Guide for Educators_**, and journal **_Make Self-Care A Priority_**. I have two more self-published books slated for release during the Summer of 2021 (this being one of them). I'm living proof that YOU CAN DO IT!

Here are some things for you to consider as you explore potential hobbies.

1. If you wrote a BOOK, what would it be about?

2. Imagine your future CAREER. What are you doing?

3. If you could be ANY PERSON for a day, who would you be and why?

    a. What do you hope to experience while being this person?

4. Write down five skills or hobbies you will try because you see value, purpose, and benefits in doing so.

1.

2.

3.

4.

5.

Dr. Gwen's Self-Care Tip:

Here are 20 ideas to get you started. What are you passionate about? There is something here for everyone. Learning a new skill or hobby can be a fun stress relieving activity, side hustle, way to stay in shape, and keep your creative juices flowing.

It is never

too late to

LEARN

something new.

YOU CAN DO IT!

Building
Dancing
Singing
Sports
Cooking/Baking
Music
Teaching
Acting/Performing
Being in Nature
Sewing
Reading
Helping Others
Arts & Crafts
Science
History
Blog/Vlog
Volunteering
Documentaries
Books
Photography

M

Everything in

moderation

with

occasional

excess.

— Neil Peart

M — Moderation

Doing everything in moderation and keeping things simple is a good philosophy to live by be it eating, social media, video games, watching TV etc. **Embrace the idea of "too much of anything is not good for you".** Use common sense when it comes to gauging when enough is enough.

What you consume has a tremendous impact on your mindset and mental health. That is why it is important to routinely assess how much of any one thing you are consuming and eliminate anything or anyone who conflicts with your well-being, dreams, and aspirations.

Social media and cell phone use are prime examples. Hear me out. If you are constantly exposed to images and stories of perfect lives, your mental health will be negatively affected. Social media should be used in a **CONTROLLED** and **LIMITED** way to share your accomplishments with friends and family, celebrate and congratulate each other on your wins, offer encouragement, or ask questions about what and how people are doing.

Social media can be an inspiring form of connection. Use social media to create a collaborative community of support and to build richer, deeper, stronger, more meaningful relationships. It should not be used as a means of comparison between the life you live and small snapshots of others' lives. Come on, let's be honest, nobody is that darn happy all the time and I'm willing to bet you he/she didn't *"wake up like THAT"*!

Dr. Gwen's Self-Care Tip:

Here are a few ways to reduce screen time. Which one is the easiest to do? Which one is the hardest? Why?

No phones during meals.

No TV during meals.

No TV before chores.

No TV in the bedroom.

No TV or phones after a scheduled time.

Track and monitor your screen time.

Studies show that **over 60%** of teens text after going to bed.

N

Ninety-nine percent

of failure

comes from people

who have a habit

of making EXCUSES.

— George Washington Carver

N – No Excuses

Teenagers do not always accept failure, take responsibility for their actions, or accept that they made a mistake with grace. Making excuses may start out innocently, after all, who likes getting in trouble and the resulting consequence. However, making excuses may quickly turn into a way to avoid responsibilities or an undesirable task. **You can easily develop a habit of blaming others for your shortcomings.** For example, it's too hard, I'm not smart enough, my little brother tore up my homework, we are poor, nobody would help me, SHE/HE told me to do it, I did not hear you say that…and the list goes on and on.

I know some of you are filled with self-doubt and you are easily intimidated by the skills, popularity, or the success of others. You may lack confidence, and struggle with self-esteem, especially if you have a learning or physical disability. But I'm here to tell you that YOU are stronger than your strongest excuse and **DESERVE** everything you secretly desire. Don't keep doing the same things and expecting different results. Life just doesn't work that way. The real world won't accept excuses for your behavior. Your parents won't accept your excuses (at least they shouldn't), your teachers won't accept them, your future boss won't accept them, and the legal system won't accept them. Stop making excuses.

Focus your energy on making changes and finding solutions to your problems instead of blaming others. Absolutely every problem has a solution. I'm not suggesting that the solution is a quick fix or easy to find. However, if you are ready to find it, it's out there. Remember, don't be afraid or too proud to ask for help.

Taking responsibility for your actions and seeking solutions to problems are critical components as you strive to gain more independence and freedom from your parents.

STOP MAKING EXCUSES!

Dr. Gwen's Self-Care Tip:

Excuses stunt your growth and the opportunity to make improvements. Here is a list of things to do LESS and MORE of to live life to the fullest.

LESS	MORE
Talking	Listening
Soda	Water
Junk Food	Salads
Complaining	Complimenting
Worrying	Meditating
Social Media	Quality Time
Frowning	Smiling
Gaming	Exercising
Hate	Love
Attitude	Gratitude

Organization isn't about

PERFECTION

it's about efficiency,

reducing stress and clutter,

saving time and money,

and IMPROVING

your overall quality of life.

— Christina Scalise

O – Organization

Organization and time management can make or break YOU during your teenage years. **Organization is an essential life skill.** When you are disorganized and do not have consistent routines, it is easy to become overwhelmed by endless responsibilities. Multiple classes, deadlines, extra-curricular activities, and other responsibilities in middle and high school as well as college can be a real challenge for some teens and is exceedingly difficult to manage. It takes time and practice to learn organization skills. Learning organization strategies can help you be more effective and efficient in getting tasks completed in a timely fashion. Organization can also be a confidence-booster once mastered.

Try these 5 Solutions to Help You Get and Stay Organized:

1. Use Your Smart Phone

Schedule due dates, with frequent reminders, in your smart phone. Take advantage of the fact that you are on your phone 24/7. Use it as a tool to help keep you organized.

2. White Board Calendar

Use your whiteboard to track assignments, due dates, extra-curricular activities, chores etc. Having a visual reminder that is readily accessible will help you stay on track.

3. Planners

Use a planner to write down assignments and events as they are announced and keep it in your backpack. The great thing about planners is that they usually have a daily, weekly, and monthly view.The various views allow you to see upcoming assignments at a glance. You can easily check tasks off as they are completed.

4. Routines

Start by creating and adhering to a basic structure for the day such as what time you will wake, eat, go to school, do activities (extracurricular, chores), and sleep. Routines can help you feel less stressed out, more organized, and in control. Of course, your schedule may change slightly depending on the day of the week but having an established routine will help you easily make adjustments.

5. Visual Organizers.

I color code everything. It's a system that I found worked for me as a child that I still use today. For example, I use color coded dividers in binders to keep topics separated at home and work. I also use color coded pens when taking notes to highlight headers, important information etc. I encourage my students to use color-coded notebooks and folders for different subjects (green is science, black is math, red isreading etc.) because it is an easy way to keep materials organized.

Dr. Gwen's Self-Care Tip:

- The best organization strategy is the one that works for you.

- Incorporate new organization strategies little by little. You don't have to do everything at once. Pick the area of your life that is most problematic and start there.

- Decide whether you prefer digital or traditional paper planners.

- Use simple office supplies to de-clutter your desk, locker, and bedroom. These supplies may include folders, pencil boxes, binder clips, storage bins etc.

- Use apps to help keep you on track with to-do lists.

P

Think

Positive,

Be

Positive,

And

Positive Things

Will Happen.

P – Positive Attitude

You are what you think, all day every day.

Be kind to yourself and think positive.

Nobody likes a Negative Nellie or a Debbie Downer.

If you focus on negative thoughts that cross your mind, then that's what you are going to start believing, so try shifting to a more positive outlook on life.

Henry Ford said, "Whether you think you can, or you think you can't – you're right."

There are many famous people who have overcome adversity. Don't make excuses or blame others for your shortcomings.

Take Michael Jordan for example. **"I've missed over 9,000 shots in my career and lost close to 300 games. Twenty-six times I've been trusted to make the game winning shot and missed. I've failed over and over and over again in my life. And that is why I succeed."**

Lebron James followed that up by saying **"Don't be afraid of failure. This is the way to succeed."** You can do whatever you put your mind to.

Dr. Gwen's Self-Care Tip:

When negative, self-defeating, sabotaging thoughts enter your mind, stop listening to them and say to yourself it is not...

True

Helpful

Inspiring

Necessary

Kind

Don't say negative things to or about others either.

Spend time with those you love.

One of these days you will say

either,

"I wish I had",

OR

"I wish I did."

— Zig Ziglar

Q – Quality Time

During your teen years is the time when you begin to spend more time with friends than family. However, your teenage years are a great time to spend doing things you enjoy with your family whether it is sitting down to eat a meal together, going for a walk, playing games, cooking, hiking, or watching a movie together. Afterall, in a few more years you will be off to college, working or both and will have less time to spend with your family. Cherish these moments while they are in abundance.

It's important to spend time with the people you love. For example, sharing a meal with your family provides an opportunity to talk about your day, to ask them about their day and to get some positive attention. Kids who feel comfortable talking to their parents about everyday things are more likely to openly talk about harder things when the time comes. Remember, no phones allowed at the dinner table.

Dr. Gwen's Self-Care Tip

Here are 5 ways to spend quality time with others.

1. Go For A Walk

Whether you are taking a walk in the park or walking around your neighborhood, walking, and talking can help relax you and strengthen the bond between you and your family. While walking, engage your senses. Take notice of the sights, sounds, smells, and the feel of nature. If you are an adventurous, outdoorsy person, consider taking a hike.

2. **Game Night**

Schedule a family game night with pizza and a variety of snacks. Few things are better than an evening filled with laughter and good ole fashioned competitive fun. That is of course if you are not a sore loser. Don't be a sore loser!

3. **Exercise Together**

Having a friend or family member next to you in the gym while you're on the treadmill, in an aerobics class, or in the weight room can help keep you motivated and accountable while spending quality time together. Exercising together also helps to keep you both in great shape!

4. **Cook A Meal Together**

One of the best ways to bond with your family is to plan, prepare and eat a meal together. Add your favorite dessert and great conversation, and you'll want to make it a regular event.

5. Volunteer Together

Serving others is always good for the mind, body, and soul. Find an organization that can always use a little help. Volunteering at a local animal shelter or food pantry will make you feel valued and appreciated. Volunteering is a great way for you and your family and friends to spend quality time while helping those in need.

Lost
time
is never
found.

R

Early to bed
and early to rise
makes a man
healthy,
wealthy,
and wise.

— *Benjamin Franklin*

R – Rest and Re-energize.

Do you struggle to get out of bed in the mornings? What about staying awake in class? Well, you are not alone. Many teenagers complain of being tired and sleepy all the time.

Scientific research shows that many teens do not get enough sleep. To be at your best, **you need between 8 and 10 hours of sleep every day**. While homework, extra-curricular activities, family time and chores make it seemingly impossible to get the recommended amount at times, it's important to try to get as much as possible.

Although getting enough sleep may not seem that big a deal, teens who don't get enough sleep and are overtired are more likely to:
- struggle in school.
- have trouble with focus and attention.
- lack motivation to complete tasks.
- have more car accidents.
- engage in risky behavior (drugs and alcohol, sex, violence).
- feel depressed, which can lead to depression.

Dr. Gwen's Self-Care Tip:

Here are a few suggestions to help you get adequate sleep:
- Go to bed at a consistent time every night.
- Sleep in your bed.

- Exercise daily.
- Avoid caffeine and energy drinks, especially in the afternoon and evenings.
- Limit exposure to electronics (computer, cellphone, kindle etc.) at least an hour before bedtime. Make sure you silence them so that you are not tempted to check them during the night.
- Keep your bedroom cool, dark, and quiet.

Talk to your parents if you are still having trouble sleeping after trying these tips.

S

It's never too late to

APOLOGIZE.

It's never too late to

say

I'M

SORRY.

S – Say I'm Sorry

There is no age limit on making mistakes. When you do something to hurt someone in words or deeds, even if it wasn't intentional, saying "I'm sorry" is the right thing to do. However, saying I'm sorry doesn't mean a thing if you don't really mean it and don't change your actions. Your apology is more meaningful and believable if in addition to apologizing you fix the mistake or promise to do better in the future.

We all do or say things at times that we regret either immediately or after we've had time to stop and think about how the person may have felt. Sometimes we are ashamed or embarrassed for what we said or did, especially if happened while we were angry, frustrated, sad or we know it's something we should not have done. You might want to consider doing something nice for the person after you apologize to show sincerity and that you value the relationship.

Dr. Gwen's Self-Care Tip:

Here are times when you may need to *Say I'm Sorry*.

- You lied.

- You stole something.

- You broke a rule.

- You accidently broke something.

- You hurt someone's feelings.

- You missed curfew.

- You didn't complete a chore.

- You insulted someone's beliefs or values.

- You show up late to an activity or event.

- You betray someone's trust or let them down.

- You inaccurately blame a person.

- You reject someone.

- If someone tells you that they were hurt by your words or actions (whether you feel it is justified or not).

The takeaway here is that if you want to build and maintain healthy relationships with friends and family, then you need **to take responsibility for your words and actions.** Your relationships have a lot to do with how happy you will be over the course of your life.

T

TRUST

is the easiest thing in the world

to lose,

and **the hardest thing** in the

world **to get back.**

- R. Williams

T – Trustworthy

Trustworthy, yeah that's the person you want to BE. Well, that is if you want to gain and maintain any semblance of freedom, independence, and privacy for the foreseeable future.

A trustworthy person is honest, dependable, and does EXACTLY **what** they are supposed to do or say they are going to do **when** they say they are going to do it with or without a handshake, fist pump, pinky promise, or someone watching over them. Like the NIKE slogan says "Just DO It!" For example, do your chores without having to be reminded. I know this might be asking a bit much but **CLEAN YOUR ROOM** too. If you can't do it daily, strive for weekly.

By keeping your word, you show that you are not only trustworthy but responsible and possess a level of maturity. Stop for a moment and think about the potential consequences of someone, specifically your parents losing confidence, faith, and trust in you. It's not a pretty picture is it? What will happen when they find out you did something you promised you wouldn't do or went some place you KNEW you weren't supposed to go with the one person you were explicitly told not be with under any circumstances?

Remember I said **your parent's primary job is to keep you safe**. If you betray their trust, that dark cloud is just going to hang around and there will be nothing but gray, gloomy, rainy days ahead. That's no fun.

Here are some sure-fire ways to lose trust and for parents to feel disrespected.

SKIPPING SCHOOL

BEAKING CURFEW

IRRESPONSIBLE DRIVING

LYING

STEALING

SUBSTANCE USE/ABUSE

SEXUAL ACTIVITY

Don't Go Nuts!

U

Never be afraid to raise your

VOICE

for honesty and truth and

compassion

AGAINST

injustice and lying and greed.

— William Faulkner

U – Use Your Voice

Using your voice at home, school, and in your community will empower you and foster a sense of purpose, belonging, value and commitment. Using your voice will also help you develop social, emotional, team building, and leadership skills. Your voice is powerful. President Barack Obama says, *"Your voice can change the world."*

Here is a great example of teenagers using their voice for change.

Parkland, Florida Shooting

On the one-month anniversary of the Parkland shootings, (when a 19-year-old former student murdered 14 students and 3 teachers with an assault rifle), students across the country **walked out of class** for 17 minutes as a silent demonstration in honor of the victims. Students were recognized for exercising their freedom of expression.

Students also organized the **March for Our Lives** in Washington, D.C. to call for reasonable gun control measures. Approximately 800,000 supporters converged on the capitol to highlight the need for gun control, while thousands more attended shadow marches in states around the country. Students used their voices to address the National Rifle Association (NRA) and politicians who take donations from the NRA while steering clear of attempts at any form of gun control.

In March 2018 Former President Barack Obama and First Lady Michelle Obama wrote a letter of support to the Parkland students which read:

> We wanted to let you know how inspired we have been by the resilience, resolve, and solidarity that you have all shown in the wake of unspeakable tragedy.

> Not only have you supported and comforted each other, but you've helped awaken the conscience of the nation and challenged decision-makers to make the safety of our children the country's top priority.

> Throughout our history, young people like you have led the way in making America better. There may be setbacks; you may sometimes feel like progress is too slow in coming. But we have no doubt you are going to make an enormous difference in the days and years to come, and we will be there for you.

Dr. Gwen's Self-Care Tip:

Here are a few examples of how YOU can use your voice for change.

VOTE

Becoming politically active and casting your vote is one of the most powerful ways you can speak out against issues that matter to you. Even if you are too young to vote, you can still play a role in elections by encouraging others to vote.

Write a letter

Writing a letter is a great way to express your thoughts and feeling about issues that impact you. Just this past year, I had a student who wrote a letter (well more of a note) to the principal about adjusting the lunch schedule so they could have a little extra recess time. His note resulted in a schedule change that not only benefited him but his entire grade level.

Organize an Event

Teenagers can help organize an event to support a cause like Unity Day, spread awareness for things like drug abuse or domestic violence, and/or advocate for change like the students you just read about from Parkland, Florida. National events that you and your peers may be interested in highlighting include National Bully Prevention Month, No One Eats Alone Day, Earth Day, and LGBTQ Activities.

Become a Leader, Advocate, and Mentor

By participating in a club, group, or organization, you have an opportunity to be a positive influence or model for others, advocate for change and develop leadership skills. Mentoring a fellow teen or a younger student struggling academically is a great way to get involved in your school or community.

What are some other ways that you can use your voice?

1.

2.

3.

4.

5.

FIND YOUR VOICE AND USE IT!

Be the CHANGE you want to see in the world!

V

VOLUNTEER!

Start where you are.

Use what you have.

Do what you can.

— Arthur Ashe

V – Volunteer In Your Community.

Your kind acts of service can have a profound impact on others, and organizations like Big Brothers, Big Sisters, and Habitat for Humanity are excellent ways for teens to put kindness into practice. Consider volunteering at one of these organizations to mentor young children or help build homes for those in need.

You might also want to consider volunteering at a local animal shelter or food bank as well. Volunteering brings joy, hope, and inspiration to others. Helping those who are less fortunate is extremely rewarding. Volunteers do not necessarily have the time; but they do have the motivation, compassion, heart, and willingness. This is an opportunity to use your **VOICE** and **TALENTS** for the common good and make the world a better place. You are never too young to change the world. We are all connected and must do our part.

Dr. Gwen's Self-Care Tip:

Audrey Hepburn once said, "As you grow older you will discover that you have two hands, one for helping yourself and one for helping others."

Here are 10 ways you can lend a helping hand:

   1. Walk a neighbor's dog.

2. Help a younger child or a struggling peer with homework.

3. Assist elderly family members or neighbors.

4. Donate old clothes, toys, or books.

5. Participate in a fundraiser.

6. Help and older person with technology.

7. Send holiday cards to service members.

8. Provide free childcare to family members or friends.

9. Assist with youth sports.

10. Participate in a park or beach cleanup.

W

Just

Drink

More

WATER

W – Water; Drink More of It.

Have you ever heard the saying...drinking water is like taking a shower on the inside of your body? Just think about that for a moment. Then ask yourself if you need to get your grimy, stinky, dirty little self in the shower or are you fresh and clean.

Getting enough water daily is important for your health. When you don't drink enough water, your body can't function at its best. It makes you more prone to **dehydration, fatigue, headaches skin problems, muscle cramps and low blood pressure.** Hydration is an energy booster. By staying hydrated, you are better equipped to deal with daily challenges. The Institute of Medicine says children and teenagers should consume about **two to three quarts of water a day** (1.7 to 3.3 liters), depending on their age, size, and sex. Other things that determine the amount of water your body needs include how healthy and active you are, and what the climate is like where you live. Boys generally need to drink more water than girls do, research suggests.

I know that 2 to 3 quarts may sound like a lot of water, but the good news is that's the total amount of water. What this means is you can count water from any beverages you drink, and foods you eat like soups, juicy fruits, and vegetables. Notice I didn't mention junk food.

Dr. Gwen's Self-Care Tip:

Here is a list of foods with their water content that you can consume to increase your water intake from healthline.com. If you're eating plenty of water-rich foods and drinking water when you feel thirsty, you shouldn't have to worry about staying hydrated.

Food	Water Content %
Lettuce	96
Cucumber	95
Zucchini	94
Tomatoes	94
Watermelon	92
Cabbage	92
Broths and Soups	92
Strawberry	91
Cantaloupe	90
Peach	89
Oranges	88
Plain Yogurt	88

When life hands you a

Xylophone

make beautiful music.

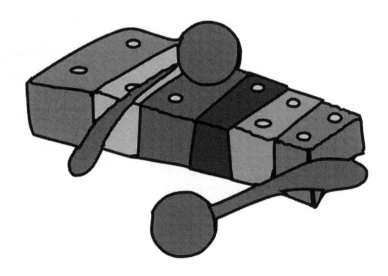

X – Xylophone.

Move with music. Music can be immensely powerful. It can magically change your mood, relate what you are feeling or simply help you relax. Music can have a profound effect on your life. Rapper Eminem says "I didn't have nothing going for me...school, home...until I found something I loved, which was music, and that changed everything." Use the space below to reflect on how music impacts your life.

Dr. Gwen's Self-Care Tip:

Music is what feelings sound like. Create a self-care playlist. These ideas will help you plan for when you are in your feelings.

Playlist Type:

1. My Favorite Artist

2. Makes me feel like dancing

3. Reminds me of someone

4. Calms me down

5. I could listen to this song all day

6. A sad song that makes me cry

7. Lifts my spirits

8. Describes me

9. Brings back fond memories

10. I can sing word for word

People haven't always been there for me, but music always was.

— *Taylor Swift*

YES

YOU

CAN

Y – YES YOU CAN

You really can make all your dreams come true. Say YES to new adventures and learning opportunities.

Richard Branson says "If someone gives you an amazing opportunity and you're not sure you can do it, say yes – then learn how to do it. Remember, that is exactly what I did when I was asked to write a chapter for the book. That's also what I call the **POWER of YET**! I try to instill this concept in my students. I do a not allow them to say they do not know how to do something without following it up with the word YET. Believing you can do something is half the battle.

Dr. Gwen's Self-Care Tip:

Create a Vision Board

One of the most powerful benefits of creating your vision board is building confidence, solidifying your dreams, and turning thoughts into possibilities.

Goal setting is important at every age and stage in your life. Creating a vision board can help you layout your ideal future using images (draw, cut, and paste), words (affirmations, quotes, phrases, slogans, graffiti), and emotions (joy, relief, peace).

Vision boards allow you to stop, think, and plan where you want to BE in life now and in the future. Visuals help to make your goals and dreams more tangible and concrete. However, a vision board is only as beneficial as the work you are willing to put into it, so be creative and open to endless possibilities as you make your vision board as thorough, exciting, and detailed as possible. **Dream BIG!** The outcome of a vision board should be a more confident, self-motivated YOU!

Z

Live a

ZIP

ZAPPY

Life!

Z – Zip Zappy

Yeah, I made this one up. Well, it is my book so I can do whatever I want. When you write your book, you can do whatever you want too. So, I'm going with ZIP ZAPPY. That's the kind of life I want to live. It means to live a life full of happiness, energy, and enthusiasm.

Life is short, and you only live once. Learning to live life to the fullest is an important step in making the most of every single day.

Here are 3 ways you can try.

1. Do What Makes You Happy

Your parents, friends, community, and society in general all have their opinions about what you SHOULD be doing. At the end of the day, you're the only person who will be around for every moment of your life. So, do more of what makes you happy. Here is the disclaimer...if it's responsible and doesn't hurt or harm YOU or others. Honor your value always.

2. Take Risk (Calculated and Informed)

Step outside the box and color outside the lines. Staying in your comfort zone will not help you grow and mature. You will cease to learn and become stagnate in both your school and personal life. Don't be that kid. There's a whole big world out there waiting to be conquered.

I know taking a risk can be scary, but it doesn't have to be. Taking risks can be something as simple as saying yes to working with a group when you would prefer to work alone. It can mean getting out there and dancing even though you haven't quite perfected the latest dance moves. Who cares! Get out there and have fun. You might just start a trend with your uncoordinated behind.

Find something new to try today and set goals beyond what you currently believe possible.

3. **Don't let the Haters Block Your Shine**

This is your life and whatever you decide to do with it in the words of Mary J. Blige is "**JUST FINE!**" There will always be someone hanging around to throw some shade by pointing out all the reasons you won't succeed or criticizing every move you make. Later for them haters.

Try your best to avoid anyone who isn't living their zip zappy best life and don't want you to live yours either. **JEALOUSY** and **INSECURITY** is alive and well. Do not let the shortcoming of others impede your road to success. Set boundaries. For example, you might say "if you are not going to be supportive, I would appreciate you keeping your opinions to yourself."

Dr. Gwen's Self-Care Tip:

Here are a three things you can start doing TODAY to make yourself zip zappier.

1. **Take a photo**

   Capture moments in your life when and where you are the happiest. If you start to lose your zappiness, take out the photo and relive those happy moments.

2. **Say NO**

   I know we previously discussed saying yes more but there are also times when you should say NO. Avoid activities that do not add meaning to your life and drain your energy, time, and motivation.

3. **Soak Up Some Sun**

   Spend some time being one with nature. It only takes a few minutes of feeling the warmth of the sun to reset your mood. I love being in my garden and have deemed it my happy place. The garden is where I'm most zip zappy.

Afterwards

Congratulations on completing Dr. Gwen's A to Z Self-Care Guide for Teens. You did it! However, this is just the beginning of your self-care journey. Self-care is a life-long commitment. Keep making yourself a priority and doing the things that bring you joy and feed your soul. I am proud of the work you are doing. You should be too!

I thoroughly enjoyed writing this book. It is my favorite so far. I started out my educational career working with teenagers, so you guys are extremely near and dear to my heart. I tried to incorporate something for everyone, no matter what area of self-care you need to improve. We are always learning and growing, and our lives are constantly changing so make adjustments to your self-care regimen as needed.

Now that you have journeyed from A to Z, I encourage you to add to the list. There is so much more that self-care could cover for each letter. For example, J for join a group. K for knowledge is power. S for say no. I am curious to know what you would have chosen for each letter. **Visit Dr. Gwen's Counselor Café website, Facebook, Instagram, or YouTube page and send me a message with feedback.** It would be amazing and greatly appreciated if you would **leave a review on Amazon or on my website** stating what you enjoyed about the book.

You will also find additional helpful resources on the website, such as my blog, where I share even more useful tips, and a shop where self-care items can be purchased.

Peace and Blessings,

Dr. Gwen

 @drgwenscounselorcafe

 @drgwenscounselorcafe

 Dr. Gwen's Counselor Cafe

Reflections

AWARENESS, GROWTH, GOALS

This is an opportunity for you to write what you learned about yourself, growth opportunities and future goals.

_____

_____

_____

_____

_____

_____

_____

Keep Going

Keep smiling, shining, and sharing your awesomeness with your friends, family, and community. I hope that you learned all kinds of valuable tips that will help you as you continue your self-care journey.

Maintain a growth mindset so that you will continue to be a life-long learner. Self-care is an on-going commitment to being the absolute best YOU! Take the information and tips that you learned from this A to Z Guide and apply them to every aspect of your life. Commit to being just a little bit better each day. Remember small consistent changes and time yield BIG results.

It does not matter how slowly you go as long as you do not stop.

— Confucius

My Commitment

Make a commitment to yourself on how you will continue your self-care journey. Writing your commitment down and sharing it with someone will make it more achievable and you more accountable. Afterwards, take the self-care pledge.

_____

_____

_____

_____

_____

_____

_____

_____

_____

_____

Teen Self-Care Pledge

I,_____,

promise to SMILE, SHINE and SHARE my awesomeness by practicing self-care. I pledge to cultivate habits that honor ME, reduce stress, and enhance my overall health and well-being. I will take time each day to invest in ME, mind, body, and spirit because I am worth it.

Signed _____

YOU
are worth your
TIME
and
ENERGY!

At the end of every month, take time to complete a self-care wellness check-up to determine if you need to make any adjustments in your daily routines.

Self-Care Check-Up			
		YES	NO
1.	Are you expressing gratitude daily?		
2.	Are you asking for help and feedback when needed?		
3.	Are you eating fresh fruits and vegetables daily?		
4.	Do you get regular exercise?		
5.	Do you get 7-8 hours of sleep nightly.		
6.	Are you taking brain breaks throughout the day?		
7.	Have you forgiven yourself and others for past mistakes?		
8.	Is your communication with others HOT (honest, open, and two-way).		
9.	Are you spending quality time with **family** and friends?		
10.	Are your refraining from risky behaviors (lying, stealing, drugs, sex).		
11.	Are you staying hydrated?		
12.	Have you learned a new skill.		
13.	Are you putting your best effort forth on assigned tasks at home and school?		
14.	Are you using positive self-talk?		
15.	Are you kind and compassionate to yourself and others?		

We all need a daily checkup from the neck up to avoid **stinkin' thinkin'** which ultimately leads to the hardening of the attitudes.

— Zig Ziglar

Acknowledgements

Thank you to all the students and parents who have inspired me over the past 20+ years of my educational career.

Students, my time with you have been most rewarding. Even on the days when you tested boundaries and of course my patience (last nerve), we learned and grew together. I used every single challenge as a growth opportunity and I'm a better teacher and counselor as a result.

Parents, you entrusted me with your child (ren) and allowed me to walk alongside you as we helped them learn and grow academically, socially, and behaviorally. I strived to establish and maintain a collaborative partnership with each of you to ensure that students demonstrated better social skills, fewer behavioral problems and academics improved. The goal was to develop lifelong learners. We are bigger, better, stronger together!

Finally, a special word of thanks goes out to my husband Carl, family, and close friends. I appreciate your continuous support, unconditional love, and heartwarming encouragement that keeps me uplifted and inspired. I'm a lucky girl.

Images via Pixabay.

~ Notes ~

~ Notes ~

~ Notes ~

~ Notes ~

Dr. Gwen's Counselor Cafe

(Additional self-care products available on Amazon or @drgwenscounselorcafe.com/shop)

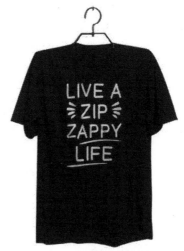

SMILE – SHINE – SHARE

TEEN HELP LINES

National Suicide Hotline
1-800-273- TALK (8255)

Crisis Textline
Text "HELLO" to 741741

Girls & Boys Town National Hotline
1-800-448-3000

Substance Abuse Mental Health Awareness National Helpline
1-800-662-HELP (4357)

National Teen Dating Violence Hotline
1-866-331-9474

Gay Lesbian Bisexual Transgender National Help Center
Youth Talkline: 1800-246-PRIDE (7743)

National Domestic Violence Hotline
1-800-799-7233 (SAFE)

45516382R00072